'A Century of Heversham

A walk in time through these old Westmorland Villages

By Malcolm Sisson

Aided by the Curwen Archives Trust

Cover photo: Toll Bar House, Ninezergh Lane, Leasgill - early 1900s

Dedicated to my wife Jennie and all the members of our family

Published by Helm Press
10 Abbey Gardens, Natland, Kendal, Cumbria LA9 7SP
Tel: 015395 61321

Copyright Malcolm Sisson 2000
First published 2000

Typeset in Transitional521BT 16pt, 10.5pt & 7pt

ISBN 0 9531836 7 X

Typeset and printed by Miller Turner Printers Ltd
The Sidings, Beezon Fields, Kendal, Cumbria, LA9 6BL Tel: 01539 740937

CONTENTS

Malcolm (me) and my wife Jennie

Hilary Hutchinson (Malcolm & Jennie's daughter)

Introduction

I was born in Sedgwick when my father was in India in the first world war. I was nearly four years old when he first saw me, although my mother sent many snapshots to India!

At five years old I went to Crosscrake School for one year, while my father was building Hill Crest, our family home in Leasgill. After moving I attended Heversham Primary School for a couple of years, and then to Milnthorpe Boys' School before going to Heversham Grammar School at age eleven.

My working life was spent at the Provincial Insurance Company in Kendal. There I met Jennie and we were married in 1941, we have three sons and one daughter and nine grandchildren.

During the war I served in the Royal Air Force working on radio and the highly secret aircraft radar installations.

I have been involved in most village activities including being closely connected with management of the Athenaeum, clerk to Heversham Parish Council, a churchwarden, local correspondent for the Westmorland Gazette, and we have both regularly attended at St Peter's Church and for many years were members of the choir.

My hobbies have mainly been gardening and photography and in younger days played tennis and badminton.

Having lived in Heversham for seventy-nine of my eighty-five years, and my family for much longer, I thought I might put on record some of the changes in the village during the last one hundred years.

I have relied mainly on my own memory and on what my father told me about the earlier years of the 20th century. I have also referred back to J F Curwen's 'History of Heversham with Milnthorpe' published in 1930; notes I made while acting as clerk to Heversham Parish Council during the years 1948–1983; and I have checked one or two dates in R D Humber's 'Heversham – The story of a Westmorland School and Village' published in 1968. The information contained is as accurate as my sources so please excuse any slight error I may have made along the way.

I would like to record my thanks to my wife Jennie, who has helped me in compiling this book, my daughter-in-law Carol for typing the manuscript, grandson William for help in preparing some of the photographs, with acknowledgement to the assistance of the Curwen Archives Trust.

Malcolm Sisson, Spring 2000

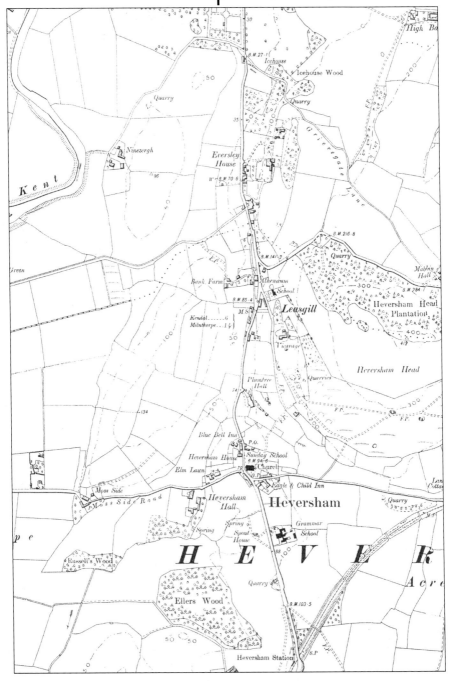

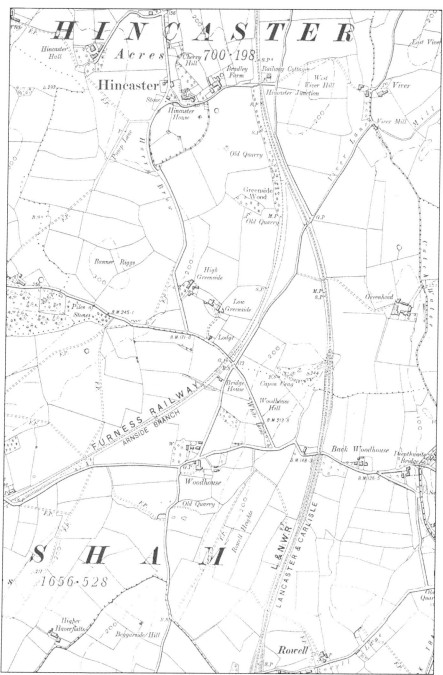

Reproduced from Second Edition 1899 Ordnance Survey Map   *Cumbria Record Office, Kendal*

Levens Bridge 1920s with the 'K' bus (owned by Bracken family) coming over. Note the AA box at the bottom of Lawrence Brow (road to Kendal). Road to the left takes you to Barrow. This photograph is looking from south to north. Note the stone at the side of the bridge to prevent carts, etc. from rubbing the wall. Levens Hall is this side of the bridge on the left.

John Marsh Photo Archive

CHAPTER ONE
LEVENS BRIDGE TO LEASGILL COTTAGE

On this walk through Heversham and its adjoining hamlet of Leasgill, we will travel from north to south, making a few diversions, and take in just a bit of Levens parish by starting from Levens Bridge.

In 1928 Levens Bridge was widened to more than twice its previous width by building a new arch on the eastern (Levens Park) side. Princes Way (of which more later) had been opened in 1927 to take the increasing volume of traffic from the village road, and the original narrow bridge became a bottleneck and dangerous. To carry out the widening work metal piles were driven into the central part of the bed of the river, to make a temporary dam while the new foundations for the central arch were put in place. An enormous steam hammer drove the piles and it was of great interest to schoolboys of my age. The lower parts of the piles were left in place and can still be seen by looking over the bridge.

On Sundays in the early days of the century, Levens Bridge used to be lined by locals on both sides – it was a regular meeting place. Kendal Cycling Club also met there before racing to the Derby Arms (near Witherslack) and back. On weekdays, picture the scene – streams of horse-drawn carts carrying potatoes from Foulshaw, damsons from Lyth, coal to Levens, flour from Milnthorpe Station to Crosthwaite, gunpowder from Sedgwick, Edward Clark's and Harold Hyde's carrier carts and Mashiter's (horse-drawn) omnibus from Milnthorpe to Kendal, also cattle and sheep being led or driven.

The Kendal Fire Brigade probably hurtled over the bridge on 3rd February 1905 to help put out a fire at Levens Hall. Miss Mary Bagot (who lived at the Hall), had given the alarm by cycling to Kendal in fifteen minutes – according to notes left by my father. He was one of the local volunteers attending the scene to deal with the outbreak.

Before leaving the bridge we will take a look at the north side. Originally this was a straight forward T-junction with the road leading to Grange and Barrow. At the junction there was a triangle of grass and a large tree in the middle. Eventually this area was raised and curbed and tarmacadamed and a seat was built round the tree, where people waited for buses to Kendal, Lancaster and Grange. With the passing of time traffic increased and the bus stops were moved to the south and west. Later the tree was cut down and the raised area became part of the road, and traffic lights were installed and continued in use for some years before the present layout was made.

For many years a black and yellow AA Box was also at the T-junction built into the wall of Levens Park, but again because of the amount of traffic this was moved to a site near the junction of the village road with Princes Way, before removed altogether.

Leaving the bridge on the left, we pass the Levens Hall estate workshop. In front of this was a large building called the Levens Welcome, a hall rather like the Leasgill Athenaeum. It was previously a barn and a bothy, (accommodation for unmarried gardeners) and was converted by Mrs Bagot of Levens Hall into a room for meetings, dances, parties, and religious services on Sunday evenings. The Heversham Brownies also met there with their Brown Owl, Miss Pamela Drew. It was here that we also took our entry forms for the Levens Flower Show held in the 1920s and 1930s. This show was held in the grounds of Levens Hall in August in two large marquees. There were the usual sections for fruit, vegetables and flowers, children's classes, and various flat races for adults and children also formed part of the event. It was a day much looked forward to by Heversham and Levens people. The Welcome had to be demolished to make way for the dual carriageway leading from the bridge.

At the end of Levens Hall garden wall we come to Ninezergh Lane on the right leading to Ninezergh, which means Ninean's Farm. This was the site of the Toll Bar House and this too was demolished around 1928 The building's function as Toll Bar had ceased long ago but I remember part of the house being used as a small sweetshop. My father used to tell the story about the occupier of the house being quite scared one morning when he went into an outhouse at the back, only to be confronted with a large brown bear and its German owner, who had apparently dossed down there for the night. Such itinerants toured the country exhibiting their bears, which would do perhaps a 'dancing' routine or other kind of performance.

Opposite is Grievegate Lane and this now overgrown bridleway with Ninezergh Lane, has formed the northern boundary of Heversham Parish since 1986. At the entrance to Grievegate, note the 1757 stone pointing the way to 'Kurby' (Kirkby). The bridleway passes the Levens Hall ice house on the left (a deep pit used previously for cold storage) and joins the road again at Mabbin Hall Farm and on to Crooklands and Kirkby Lonsdale.

Moving on and up the hill we pass the gates to Eversley, a large house built for the Argles family and completed in September 1859 and enlarged in 1904. The Argles family were the 'gentry' and owned much of the land, farms and

Toll Bar House with Ninezergh Lane just beyond on the left. The small roofed building at the end of Levens Hall garden wall was the gardeners' smoking shed. The entrance to Grievegate Lane is on the right. The man on the left is Mr Latham - early 1900s.

Eversley, the home of the Argles family as it was early in the 1900s. Today the house is divided into four separate houses.

Wedding photo of Mr T A Argles of Eversley to Miss Agnes Wakefield of Sedgwick House.

Mrs Argles of Eversley 'Leasgill Band' c.1903 (J H Hogg photo)
Back row second left: 'Botanical Tom' Mason; fourth along from left Proctor Birkett (Leasgill)
Middle row first left: Edward Powley, Greengate Farm, Levens (First to be baptised in Heversham Church); third
along on left Mrs A Argles (Agnes Wakefield); fifth from left Mary Powley (Greengate).
Front row: middle is Harriet Sisson of Heversham and on the right Agnes Powley. *John Marsh Archive Collection*

12

cottages in the village. The family did much for the benefit of the village. Mrs Agnes Argles was the sister of Mary Wakefield, the founder of the music festival held in Kendal. Agnes ably assisted Mary in musical matters and she herself founded the Heversham and Levens Choral Union, and when choirs from Milnthorpe and Beetham were added in 1912, it became known as the Eversley Choral Union, which is still a highly regarded choir. About 1903 Mrs Argles also conducted the 'Leasgill Band of Servants and Tradesmen'. This was a group of about fifteen stringed instrument players. One tradesman member was Tom Mason, violinist, who had a Temperance Bar (non-alcoholic), in Highgate, Kendal (next to the present Kendal Bowman). Another was Proctor Birkett, double bass, a Leasgill coachman. Edward Powley and Mary Powley of Levens, played the cello and violin. My Aunt Harriet Sisson of Leasgill was also one of the violin players. Mr Frank Argles provided the village with the Athenaeum, about which more later.

About 1927 Eversley was bought by John M Drew, a cotton magnate from Lancashire, he and his family took over the house, altered it and added to it. Unfortunately Mr Drew died early and the family moved first to Eversley Lodge which had been the chauffeur's house, and subsequently to High Leasghyll, formerly the parish vicarage. Eventually, Eversley was divided into four separate houses and new houses were also built in the garden. Part of the area had been a rather splendid Japanese garden while the Drew family occupied the house. This garden was built on or near the old tennis courts which were used by Heversham Ladies' Tennis Club when the Argles family owned Eversley. The club later moved to courts near Plumtree and became a mixed club.

In the field opposite the Eversley gateway, there was a well from which water was pumped literally by horsepower to a large tank under part of the Athenaeum. Village people were allowed to take their drinking water from the tank. This was before piped water from Lupton Tarn was brought to the village about 1908. The small door on the west side of the Athenaeum enclosing the tap can still be seen.

Most of the houses in Leasgill belonged to the Eversley Estate, their staff, such as the chauffeur, butler and gardener, occupied some. Eversley Farm (also known as Home Farm and Croft Farm at one time) was a fully working farm, where I as a boy often went to collect our milk in two milk cans, one for full cream and the other for 'blue' milk, now called fully skimmed milk. The cream removed was made into butter in the farm dairy by Mrs Strickland, the farmer's wife. This was common practice on most farms until wartime. All the barns and outbuildings have now been converted to dwellings.

As we walk up towards Mabbin Hall Lane we pass Leasgill Cottage which had a large orchard, but this is now part of the adjoining field. When the Eversley butler lived here and the orchard was in full production, we were given lots of pears which were delicious stewed with stick cinnamon. This house was once a school for young ladies and was so successful that classes had to be held in the Athenaeum. The school closed in 1906.

Opposite the house is the stone which marked the boundary between Heversham and Levens until 1986. The boundary went right through the house, so occupants dined in Levens and went to bed in Heversham.

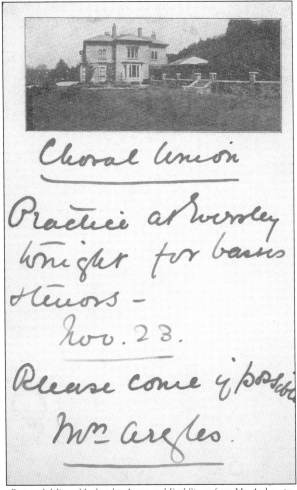

Post card delivered by hand to James and Fred Sisson from Mrs Argles - to attend band practice.

CHAPTER TWO
PLANE TREE COTTAGE TO THE ATHENAEUM

The house just beyond the boundary stone is Plane Tree Cottage. There is no plane tree here, but there is a large sycamore tree within the garden. In Scotland and the north of England the sycamore is also known as the plane tree. This tree must be very old – it seems to have hardly changed since the 1920s. Plane Tree Cottage was in the early 1900s the home of the Eversley gardener.

At this point the 'Low Road' leaves the village road on the right. This was the main road through the village until 1801. In the 1920s there was a 5 mph sign which the few motorists at that time were expected to obey. The road is now only two hundred and eighty-five yards long but it used to continue in front of Ghyll Cottage, Dunloe and Yew Tree Cottage.

Our family house, Hill Crest, is just a hundred yards up Mabbin Hall Lane, my father built this in 1920/21 and a separate wing was added by my brother in 1976.

The small area of land between the Low Road and the village road contains the Athenaeum, which until 1872 was my great grandfather's barn and joiners workshop. The Athenaeum, provided as a (*) 'room for penny readings' for the villagers by Frank Argles, has been a great asset to the village for one hundred and twenty-seven years. (*This was a room or hall where village people could go to read books and newspapers and generally educate themselves and also somewhere to meet socially. There was probably a charge of one penny per night).

Mr Argles was a member of the Athenaeum Club in Liverpool (not the one in London) and he decreed that the name should also apply to the new room for penny readings. Most villages have a village hall, but Heversham is unique in having an Athenaeum.

The Athenaeum had its first update in 1927, when the stage was moved from the east end of the main hall to the west (and other improvements made), and again in 1985 with new kitchen and toilet facilities, and more recently in 1998 when the main hall was vastly improved, the stage removed and the main entrance now coming from the car park. This is the fourth time the main door has been moved anti-clockwise round the building!

The car park (originally the garden belonging to Leasgill House) was purchased in 1979. A further development at the Athenaeum was the

Leasgill – before 1920. Looks rather like present time. Ghyll Cottage (formerly Laundry Cottage) and Dunloe Cottage on the left with Highfield facing on the right. The small road off to the left is the original road through the village and note the 'VR' letter box at junction. The larch tree on the left and the sycamore on the right, were felled in the second half of the 20th century.

Athenaeum with Highfield just showing on the right. This was taken in 1985 after the car park was made and before modernisation began.

creation of a snooker room by transforming the old stabling and coach house on the basement level. The new snooker room was opened in October 1994. The Athenaeum continues to be well used by village organisations, including the indoor bowling club, the Women's Institute, old time dancing, badminton, art lessons, yoga and two lecture societies – Forum and Quest. The Athenaeum finally became parish property by Deed of Gift from the Argles family in 1927.

During wartime the Athenaeum was used as an 'overflow' from the primary school when evacuees came to the village from Barrow-in-Furness and Tyneside areas. The hall was used for teaching and as a canteen, the latter continuing for some time after the war. Until the primary school had its own hall in 1999 children used it for gymnastics and games.

Much earlier in the century the Athenaeum housed the village library, the library room being open one or two nights a week and very dim it seemed with only a small oil lamp for illumination. Nevertheless, the library was much used and appreciated when transport to Kendal Library was very limited. Books were also sent down from Kendal by carrier's cart in large wooden boxes and exchanged for new supplies regularly. The library continued for most of the first half of the last century after which it operated for some years from the Old School and eventually the mobile library van took over.

Children in playground practising the 'Singing Game' entered in Mary Wakefield Festival - 'King of the Barbarees' - about 1929.
Left to right standing - Jean Park, Gladys Hayton, Jean Binnie, Paddy Chapman, Edna Hayton, Edward Sisson, Ruby Nelson, Nancy Whitwell, Ray Sisson, Edith Binnie, R Sisson
Phyllis Wills and Evelyn Halliwell.

CHAPTER THREE
OTHER LEASGILL PROPERTIES UP TO PLUMTREE

The first of the other three houses on the narrow strip north of the Athenaeum (Valley View) was built in 1923. This area was a copse of mixed trees where bees were kept. The land was cleared to make way for the other two houses (Holly Bank and Overdale) built in the early 1960s.

On the opposite side of the road, note the small two-storey building in the garden of Highfield. This house was built in 1896 and the nearby houses of Underwood and Leasgill Brow followed soon after. Leasgill Brow was once occupied by Mr Alfred Binyon who gave lantern lectures in the Athenaeum on travel, poetry and architecture. He was a scholarly man and a relative of Laurence Binyon, (poet and art critic who worked at the British Museum during the years 1893-1923), whose immortal words "They shall grow not old as we that are left grow old. Age shall not weary them nor the years condemn. At the going down of the sun and in the morning we will remember them," are spoken all over the land on Remembrance Sunday. Underwood was the home of Mr and Mrs W Nelson. Mrs Nelson was for many years organist at St Peter's Church and a leader in musical activities for both adults and children in the village. The Orchards and Woodland Hall are infillings and were built in 1968 and 1974.

To return to the small two-storey building, this was the tailor's workshop used by Mr John Germain who lived at Highfield in the early years of the century. Mr Germain and his assistant Frank Birkett (who eventually took over the business) made suits to order and did repairs. They sat cross-legged on a low platform in the upper window with needle and thread in hand. The lower room was the shop where boys from Heversham Grammar School went to buy their school caps and blazers. In later years the building was used as an art studio, a tobacco store, a dressmakers workshop, an electricians store and for a few weeks as a small tea-room by my granddaughter Jenny. Now the premises are used as an office.

The lane opposite the east side of the Athenaeum leads to the Primary School which opened in 1871 and replaced the Old Girls' School near the church. In my school days most boys left this school at about age of eight and went to Milnthorpe Boys School (now a private house) near the comb mill. Teaching at Leasgill was somewhat old fashioned and pupils had little prospect of gaining entry to the Grammar School. At Milnthorpe we felt we had more chance. Soon after 8 o'clock about ten or a dozen of us would set

Heversham girls' primary school (1838) and school mistresses house (1841), with churchyard in front.

Later primary school in lane opposite Athenaeum which opened 1891.   (Picture taken in 1996).

J Sisson

off walking to Milnthorpe, generally kicking a ball on the way – there was little road traffic so it wasn't really dangerous. If we were very lucky we hitched a lift on the back of a coal lorry.

A little later boys usually chose to go to Levens School and this continued for some time before our Primary School attained its present excellent teaching standards. The Primary School has had various updates and extensions over the last century and a much needed school hall was built and opened in 1999 by the Rt Reverend Ian Harland, Bishop of Carlisle. The hall is known as the John Hancock Hall and it provides excellent facilities for indoor games, assemblies and gymnastics.

Further up the lane we come to High Leasghyll. This was the vicarage until 1947, when under the will of Mrs Rhoda Thompson, her residence known as 'The Knoll' in Woodhouse Lane, was bequeathed to the parish for use as a vicarage. Reverend Wilfred Alec Cleghorn was the first Heversham vicar to use the new vicarage. When Miss H. Drew lived at High Leasghyll this was the headquarters of a very successful Girl Guide Troop, later taken over by Mrs Betty Tyson. Alas, no one came forward to take over after her retirement.

The school lane goes further to Heversham Head Quarry – now disused and overgrown - but here at one time village people could remove stone for building etc. This limestone quarry is jointly owned by Heversham and Milnthorpe. This stems from the years before 1896 when separate parish councils were formed for Heversham and Milnthorpe. Before that date the ancient parish of Heversham included Milnthorpe, as well as Preston Patrick, Sedgwick and Stainton, Levens and Crosthwaite.

Almost adjoining, is the old Grammar School founded in 1613 and the open-air cockpit on its eastern side (cock fighting became illegal in 1849). This building has fallen into disuse but was used last century as a hen house, Scout Headquarters and an art centre. In the field below is Plumtree Bank, once the headmaster's house, but in the early 1900s was the home of the gardener and chauffeur employed at Plumtree Hall.

The field below the old Grammar School used to be the site of the Plumtree Hall tennis court. The Misses Watson allowed the court to be used by the Heversham Tennis Club which flourished for many years. The single court proved inadequate for the number of members and a second court was made, but this in turn became a bowling green, which lasted only a few seasons. After the war young people tended to leave the village for college or university. The few older tennis players found it difficult to keep the club going and the whole area became part of the adjoining field. A seat on the west side of Plumtree garden wall was put there in 1965 by the Womens Institute, to

Tennis Court converted for a short time as a bowling green. Miss Watson opening with rolling the first bowl with Frank Senogles - 1930s. Also present are: Frank Dickinson - proprietor of Heversham Hotel - (standing on the left with hands in his pockets); James Duncan (folded arms) and Hermione Drew dressed all in white. *Jean Simpson*

celebrate the Golden Jubilee of the national body (not the local WI which began in 1927).

Retracing our steps to the village road, note the 'V R' letterbox in the wall at the end of the car park – over a hundred years of constant use. A little further on the right is Ghyll Cottage formerly called Laundry Cottage, because village people were allowed to bring their laundry to be mangled and ironed in the room reached by the external steps. Opposite are the two new Milestone Cottages built on land previously used as allotments. The adjacent house, High Rise, dates from 1967 and then we come to three new houses, built in 1995/96 on the site of the joiner's workshop which existed there since the 1870s.

James Sisson, a Kendal joiner, moved to Leasgill in 1833, and until about 1870 used the buildings which now constitute the Athenaeum as his workshop. He was given permission in 1865 at a meeting of local ratepayers to erect a wooden shed on the township waste land in Leasgill, and the family continued the undertaking, joinery and wheelwright's business there until late in the century, when John Hodgson took over the buildings for his own joinery business. Subsequently the land was sold for housing development – permission for a row of small cottage homes was refused and the larger houses built instead. The name 'Applegarth' derives from part of the site having been a garden and orchard. Before the houses were built a small amount of spring water ran into a stone trough on

Ancient open air cockpit, Heversham, with old Grammar School in background - 1990   *J Sisson*

The old joiner's workshop Three modern houses were built in 1995/6 on the site of my great grandfather's workshop. This photograph was taken just before the houses were built.

Victory Row 1906 - with families standing outside. There were four houses, later on two were made into one, now called West View, Underhill and West Cottage.

Photo left - Mrs Strickland and three daughters - Martha, Sarah and Annie.

Middle - James Sisson (my father in rolled up poner's apron), Harriet Sisson (my aunt with the dog) Maggie Wilson (niece of above brother and sister).

Right - Mrs Proctor holding Lily Proctor, Mary Proctor and Mr Proctor. Geoffrey Medcalfe (end of doorway), two Proctor boys and Tommy Thompson.

Note poster on notice board advertising Liberal Demonstration - time of the great Liberal revival.

R. Sisson

the roadside where Applegarth House stands. At times of heavy rain the water overflowed across the road and into the Haysteads field on the north side of Rose Cottage. Could this be the remains of the original Leas Gill? The stone trough was retained and repositioned on the roadside a little to the north.

The next row of houses on the left was once known as Victory Row. Part of the first of these was a paint store used in connection with the joiner's workshop, and after that used as a garage and repair shop and a battery charging station, at the time when most radios ('wireless sets' then) needed electric accumulators to provide the power. Mr Frank Park, the proprietor, used a large motorcycle and box sidecar to collect and deliver the batteries to many houses in the parish area. A recharge was needed every two weeks or so. Mr Park had a small petrol engine and generator to provide the power.

The first 'wireless set' in Leasgill was installed at Underwood, opposite the Athenaeum, then occupied by Mr and Mrs W Nelson. This would be in the mid 1920s. I think Mr and Mrs Nelson's son, John had the set given by an uncle and I remember being fascinated by sound coming from the horn-type loudspeaker. The set was a wooden box with a sloping front panel on which glowing valves were mounted with dials and coils. We are used to seeing television aerials now but the early wireless set needed a long outdoor aerial. This consisted of a copper wire between the chimney pots or from a chimney to a tall pole about twenty metres away in the garden and there was a 'downlead' from the aerial to the set, which went through the window-frame and an 'earthlead' which came out to a metal plate or pipe in the ground. Gradually aerials began to appear on more and more houses and remained on some properties until after the war. A radio set can now be operated by the flick of a small switch, but in the early days very careful adjustment of several controls was needed to 'tune in' to the station you wished to hear.

Parks' Garage, as it was widely known, was also the main bus stop in Leasgill. A regular bus service from Lancaster to Kendal began in 1922, operated by Lambsfields. After several changes, including a spell as Cumberland and Westmorland Motors, this became Ribble Motor Services and eventually Stagecoach. The Fawcett family of Milnthorpe also operated the Dallam buses between Kendal and Arnside. There was considerable competition between the rival services, Dallam often running five or ten minutes in front of the other services. Cars had not become common and buses were often filled to capacity, standing passengers being packed like sardines down the gangway. As an example of fares, Leasgill to Kendal return was 11d (5p) and a weekly Dallam ticket cost 2/11d (15p). For a short time there was also a third bus service – the 'K' buses running between Kendal and Lancaster, and Kendal and Grange, but this service

Haysteads pond. This pond had to be drained when Princes Way was made. This photo is pre-1920. Note the hawthorn trees – lanterns were hung in them for skating in winter after dark.   *R Sisson*

Construction of Princes Way - opened 1st July 1927. Mr Kerr, clerk of works, standing dressed in suit near centre of picture. He and his family lodged with us at Hill Crest.   *John Marsh Photo Archive*

Leasgill from Princes Way soon after the road was opened and before the trees were planted. The small filling station on the corner of Haysteads field can be seen. This section of the road was originally concrete – now covered over.

Petrol Station, Princes Way - early 1930s. Standing from left James Thompson (great uncle); Frank Varley (proprietor); Mr Booth(?) retired farmer; Malcolm Sisson (myself); Harold East and Mrs Varley (mother of Frank). Norah Varley (sister of Frank) is sitting in the car.

never seemed to have the success of the others. The 'K' slogan was – 'by day the bus with a big K, by night the bus with the blue light'. The Dallam bus service was taken over by Ribble company in 1950.

Opposite Applegarth is one of Leasgill's oldest houses, Yew Tree Cottage; a tailor lived here in 1737. The larger Yew Tree House is much later in date and stands on part of the original Low Road. Next in line is Rose Cottage, another old property, but updated during the last century, and this is followed by the newer Strickland House, the date of 1876 being carved into the stonework.

The next group of five houses on the left are all modern, built in more recent years on what we used to call the hayfield. The daffodils which cover the grassy bank were planted to celebrate the Golden Jubilee of the Westmorland Federation of the Women's Institute in 1968 and have been a springtime spectacle ever since. The houses look across to Haysteads, a drumlin containing deposits of granite brought down from Shap in the ice age. Some of this had to be cut away when Princes Way was made in 1926/27 and a large pond at the foot of Haysteads had to be drained. The making of Princes Way put an end to both an excellent toboggan run down the hill and over the pond when frozen and to local ice skating.

Princes Way was constructed by the Irlam firm of Monk & Company. Moving large amounts of earth and stone would not have been a big problem with the use of today's massive machines but then it was mainly pick and shovel work. There was, however, a small gauge railway with trucks and engines to move the excavated earth to parts of the route which needed filling in. An exciting scene for school boys! The by-pass was originally planned to end at the north side of Plumtree, keeping traffic away from the dangerous church corner. Fortunately the route was extended thus keeping the whole village clear of through traffic.

The new road was built largely through the efforts of John F Curwen, then Chairman of the Heversham Parish Council, who drew the attention of the County Council to the dangerous church corner. The County Council eventually agreed that the new road should completely replace the existing narrow and tortuous road through Heversham and Leasgill. Princes Way was opened on 1st July 1927 by HRH Prince of Wales (later Edward VIII). The short ceremony was watched by a large crowd: the Prince used golden scissors to cut a white satin ribbon and then made the first official use of the new highway.

Soon after the Princes Way was opened a small petrol station was built for Mr Frank Varley (son of the village blacksmith), at the northern end of Haysteads field. Mr Varley was severely disabled and boys were glad to help

Bank Farm 1970s. This was a working farm when the photograph was taken. The filled milk kits were placed on the stand, collected daily and taken to the Milk Factory at Milnthorpe.

Land army girls - on right is Peter Handley. Pictured having a well earned tea break from potato picking on land west of village. Haysteads and Heversham Head in background.   *Jean Simpson*

in turning the hand-operated pumps. There were three pumps at first, each delivering a different brand of petrol – BP, Shell and National Benzole. Petrol stations were not then tied to one supplier. Later a fourth pump was added and the price of petrol in the 1930s was about 11½d (5p) per gallon. Mr Varley ran the business for many years and it was then taken over by one of the national networks and much enlarged. This in turn closed and now we have four industrial units.

Before we leave Leasgill, another small detour takes us to the west side of the Athenaeum and the small lane leading to Princes Way. Before the by-pass was made this led only to Leasgill Lodge (our home for 30 years) and to Bank Farm and thence via a footpath to College Green Lane. Leasgill Lodge had a large garden but no modern conveniences. When we went there in 1946 after my demobilisation from the RAF, there was only a single cold water tap and sink and an old fashioned farmhouse style range, with a broken boiler. The corner of the kitchen was taken up by an old fashioned copper boiler for washing clothes. Most houses had one of these either within the dwelling or in an outhouse. We had to be up early on washing days to light the boiler fire, to boil the clothes before transferring them to a large galvanised tub where they were agitated with dolly legs before being put through the mangle with large wooden rollers. How times have changed! The privy was outdoors down the garden path. Building materials were scarce and restrictions on spending were

Mr Jimmy Frear with Benny and Chessey at Bank Farm.

strict in the first years after the war, but we gradually made our home very comfortable. Eventually, we built Hazelrigg at the top of the garden and moved there in 1975.

Bank Farm was a fully working farm run on rather old-fashioned lines and never became mechanised. Horses were used for ploughing, carting etc. Milk was collected in large 'kits' from the farm gate and taken to the Milnthorpe milk factory. (Milk kits were cylindrical metal containers, narrowing at the top end where the lid was fastened. Each kit contained about twelve gallons of milk). The barns were in full use storing hay (pre-silage days) and corn, and the threshing machine visited once a year. The farm was run by Diana and Hermione Drew, with their farm manager Jimmy Frear and Land Army girls.

Mr Frear was a true Westmorland character, generally conversed in dialect and loved by all, including children, especially when he invited them to have a ride on the horse and cart. In course of time farming ceased and today the Armers have converted the farm into a couple of houses, an office, a workshop and a showroom for the family business, Panararmer

Just before reaching Plumtree Hall we come to Plumstones and The Whins. These houses were added to the village in 1973 and 1975.

The annual visit of the travelling threshing machine at work at Bank Farm in the 1970s.

31

Hooping a wheel. Local wheelwrights brought wooden cart wheels to Heversham Smithy to have the iron tyre fitted. The tyre was fashioned by the smith and heated in a ring of burning peat to expand it slightly. It was then slipped over the wooden wheel and quickly hammered into place. Water was poured on the rim to prevent the wood burning. Picture shows Harry Varley (smith) with hammer raised, James Sisson (wheelwright) opposite and John Tarves (innkeeper from Blue Bell next door) with watering can in hand.

Chapter Four
Plumtree to Heversham House

Plumtree Hall was built c.1815 and was a private house until 1971, latterly the home of the Watson family, who were much involved in helping village activities and opened the grounds for garden fetes in aid of charities. Plumtree was one of the houses which generated its own electricity long before the grid brought light and power c.1934. The lower part of Plumtree Mews housed a petrol engine and generator, and the upper part was the room housing perhaps fifty large accumulators, supplying the house with direct current.

After 1971 the premises and large garden were bequeathed under the will of Miss Lilian Watson to be made into a retirement home and the Plumtree Housing Association was formed. As this is a listed building not much could be done to change the external appearance of the building, but a conservatory was added and opened on 24th April 1994, and outbuildings at the rear converted into extra accommodation. Most of the garden was sold off and two new homes were built. In the Watson's time, mistletoe grew prolifically on the apple trees in the orchard and there was a large alpine scree garden.

The two houses on the left just beyond Plumtree are built on what was the kitchen garden of Heversham House, Lyngarth first in 1970, followed by Maraiken in the 1990s. Opposite these is the Children's Playground, which was opened in 1974 by Brigadier Tryon-Wilson of Dallam Tower. This has

Plumtree Hall - 1908

33

been a great asset to the village providing a safe playing space for younger children. The provision of the playground arose from some years of pressure by village people and eventually the Parish Council took up the project. The Rowan tree near the gate was planted by Ray Sisson, then President of the Women's Institute, when that organisation sponsored the Cumbrian Best Kept Village entry and won first prize c.1980.

Notice the square shaped 'hole in the wall', now ivy covered. This housed the village fire-fighting equipment in a large wooden box for many years. I don't remember it being used to fight a fire! A full Fire Brigade of volunteer residents was formed in 1912. Sometime later there was a disinclination to turn out, but in 1924 J F Curwen of Horncop offered the men supper and sixteen turned up! The Fire Brigade was taken over by South Westmorland District Council in 1940, but the hose was retained and later kept in the box mentioned above.

The next buildings on the right are an interesting group steeped in history. First we come to a workshop and store which was the village smithy for very many years. Harry Varley was the smith - he was kept busy making iron goods, shoeing horses and making iron tyres, then fitting them to new and repaired cart wheels, which were brought to the smithy by local wheelwrights.

The next two houses were the original Blue Bell Inn – high on the northern gable the advertising board is still attached but is almost indecipherable. It seems to read "Blue Bell. Good accommodation, Livery(?). A choice selection of Ales, Wines and Spirits. Good stabling." The reference to the innkeeper's name is not decipherable but the tenant from 1898 was John Tarves and he continued until 1950. The licence was eventually transferred to Heversham Hotel on Princes Way which then became the new Blue Bell.

The original Blue Bell was the headquarters of Leasgill United Association Football Club, formed, I think, in 1902 (my father was the secretary). Senior members paid a subscription of 1/6d (7½p) per season and boys paid 6d (2½p). There were nearly fifty members and supporters. Matches were played against local villages, Kendal and Barrow. Not many were won, according to the record book! Accounts show the rent of the ground as £1.10s.0d (£1.50), but there is no record of where the matches were played. A new football cost 8/8d (about 45p) and twelve shirts cost £1.4s.0d (£1.20). The referee was paid 4/- (20p) per match. The club seems to have ceased to function c.1905.

Opposite the workshop and store are a group of four houses originally built as council houses in 1952 but now in private occupation. The land was previously a field entered by a gate from the road. Part of the route of the Grammar School fell race went through this gate, winding its way to the top

The old Blue Bell. John Tarves on right, with his two daughters and their dog - tenant from 1898 to 1950.

The Post Office. A first world wartime photo of the Post Office at Smithy Cottage. Mrs Varley and her daughter Nora, selling produce for 'sandbags for soldiers'.

Just showing on the right is St Mary's Well, next the Heversham Metal Industry and Post Office. The Metal Industry showroom was built in 1914, but was removed about 1928 after Princes Way was made, when cars no longer came through the village and stopped to make purchases. The foundations remain.

of Heversham Head and returning via Woodhouse Lane. I remember running this tough course several times. Brackendale, the house nearby, was built in 1956. Then we have Smithy Cottage where blacksmith, Mr Harry Varley and his family lived. This was also the Post Office during the years 1894-1923, Mrs Varley being the postmistress.

Next to the cottage are the steps leading up to the Old (Girls) School and headmistress's house. The school opened in 1842 and continued until the present Primary School was opened in 1891 which was for girls and boys. During the last century the Old School building was used for various parish and church meetings. When the village had a scout troop and brownie pack this was also their meeting place. It was also the room where the Heversham Metal Industry made artistic articles of copper and brass. The industry was established in 1891 by Mr P J Hibbert of Plumtree Hall, and continued under the Misses Watson when they came to the Hall.

Men and boys hand-made vases, jugs, trays, candlesticks, mirrors, etc. Patterns were traced onto the metal sheets and the design cut into the brass or copper with a very small chisel and a special hammer, and a decorative background added. We made useful pocket money in this way. It was reported in the Kendal Mercury and Times on 13th June 1913, that Queen Alexandra purchased a coal scuttle when she visited the Heversham Metal Industry stall, at an exhibition in the Royal Albert Hall. From 1914 the

Items made at the Metal Industry. These items were loaned by village people for an event in church in 1983.

merchandise was displayed in a small showroom at the top of the steps, looked after by the postmistress nearby. Sales were made to passing motorists until Princes Way was opened, when almost overnight, sales fell away and the showroom was taken down and no more articles were made. The foundations of the showroom can still be seen.

In the corner of the churchyard nearby, there was a gas generating plant to supply gas for lighting the church. This was in the years before electricity came to the village around 1934. The gas plant was rather like a miniature version of the cylindrical gas-holders which were seen in most towns. The gas was generated by the action of water on the chemical calcium carbide. A controlled trickle of water was allowed to enter the carbide chamber and the acetylene gas produced was stored in the gas holder.

I sometimes helped my godfather, Robert Squire the church clerk, to light the many suspended lamps. We used a taper on a special long pole with a hook to turn the tap, then lighting the burners. After the service we went round again turning the gas off! It was a joy when electric lighting was installed by the Astley family of Greenside. The lighting was updated with elegant new fittings and low energy bulbs in 1986, in memory of church warden, John Sowerby and his wife.

Heversham House - owned at one time by H J Austin of Austin & Paley architects - taken early 1900s.

On the other side of the churchyard wall by the roadside is St Mary's Well. This was a village drinking water supply before piped water arrived c.1908. The well had an Appleby pump to raise the water and this could also be diverted to a nearby trough, for use by horses and cattle. The water also came to be used by steam haulage vehicles, but in 1905 a notice was put up prohibiting this, as not enough water was left for village people. Later the pump was removed and a heavy square iron cover with a lock was put over the well. Much later again the cover was taken away and the present imitation pump put in place. Before piped water was laid on from Lupton Tarn, the Parish Council conducted a postcard referendum asking householders to indicate whether they would want the new supply. Surprisingly more than half said no, or only if it were not too expensive. Houses had large tanks to collect rainwater for washing clothes, etc and a few had their own wells. Fortunately, the water supply came and was soon accepted as normal.

We now walk across the road to Heversham House. This was bought by H J Austin (of the well-known Austin & Paley church architect firm) in 1900 and his two daughters continued to live there until well after the second war. The Misses Austin were keen gardeners and during wartime, the garden was often opened to the public to support charities such as the Red Cross. For some years in the 1960s, Heversham House was occupied by Messrs French Construction as an administrative centre, while the Brettargh Halt – Crooklands link road, was being made and the garden became neglected. About 1970 the house was sold to Heversham Grammar School and used as a boarding house until 1987. Afterwards part of the garden was sold off for buildings and in 1988 the house opened as a residential retirement home.

St Peter's Church - taken early 1900s. The sign directs people to the Eagle and Child Inn and advertises 'Good accommodation for cyclists. Good Stabling.'

CHAPTER FIVE
SAINT PETER'S CHURCH

Much has been written about St Peter's Church and it has remained unaltered outwardly through the last century. Inside some re-arrangements have been made during the last twenty-five years. The children's corner which was created in 1943 became a small separate chapel in 1981; Dallam Chapel has become the refreshment area; part of the south aisle has been altered to accommodate the music group, and a part of the north aisle became the choir vestry and space for toddlers.

The Argles family left their mark on the building, assisting with the rebuilding of the tower in the 19th century. The west window installed in 1924 is in memory of Thomas and Agnes Argles after their death in 1923 and the window depicts Saint Chad and St Thomas a' Beckett, in the left panel and Saint Ursula (Patron Saint of Women) and Saint Cecilia (Patron Saint of Music) in the right panel. The font cover installed in 1924 is also in their memory and was given by past and present parishioners. The cover is in the form of a wooden spire one hundred and fifty-two centimetres high, and is richly carved and decorated, including four winged angels.

There have been six incumbents during the last century – Canon Gilbert continued in office until 1921, followed by Reverend E R Ellis until 1939, Reverend W A Cleghorn until 1955, Canon Stanley Lane until 1964 and Reverend Tom Martin until 1976, when the present incumbent Reverend Canon John Hancock came to the parish.

Early in the 20th century, Heversham Grammar School boarders were required to attend church twice on Sundays, when dress was Eton suits and mortar board hats - which were worn flat on the head, or slightly tilted, or fully tilted to the side, or carried in the hand, according to the Sunday in the month. The initials of some of these boarders can still be seen carved into the pews. Some of the boys became members of the choir from time to time.

Two flower vases adorned the alter until the mid 1920s when an ornate brass cross and candlesticks were presented to the church. This did not meet with universal approval and they were removed and hidden behind a gravestone in the churchyard. Fortunately they were recovered undamaged and continued in use for many years, until for security reasons they were replaced by a wooden cross and candlesticks made by Ruben Askew, a talented craftsman who lived in the village.

The church bells have been rung for centuries. The present peal was installed in 1870 but became very worn and an inspection made in 1976 found various defects. In 1978 the bells were taken down and transported to Loughborough for repair and retuning. The rehanging was completed on 21st March 1978 and the bells re-dedicated on 2nd July 1979, by the Bishop of Penrith

An interesting custom in church which survived until the 1930s was the distribution of loaves of bread after morning service. An ancient charity provided for the loaves to be given out to poor and elderly people in the parish. The loaves were placed on shelves near the front and church wardens distributed them as people went out of church. I remember one lady collecting several loaves in a pillowcase.

The style of worship in church has altered very much during the last century. For much of the period we had Early Communion at 8.00am, Matins at 10.30am, sometimes followed by a Communion Service, and Evensong at 6.30pm. Once a month in the afternoon there was a children's service; in other weeks there was a Sunday School which was held in the Primary School, with three or four separate classes and teachers. This routine gradually gave way to Matins being dropped, and all the services, except a monthly Family Service, being Holy Communion, following the pattern of the Alternative Services Book for main services and the Prayer Book Service still being used at 8.00am. A bi-monthly Evensong is now held and a Praise and Worship Service once a month.

The type of music has changed from organ only and the singing of canticles, psalms and hymns, to the present use of a young people's instrumental group, with fewer ancient and modern hymns and much more Mission Praise type of singing. Sunday School ceased for a time, was revived as Fish Club (the outline of a fish being an ancient Christian symbol) on Tuesday afternoons in the Athenaeum for a short period and now the Old School is used for Sunday School on three Sundays a month.

Dress for church-going has also become much less formal. Up to the middle of the last century one rarely, if ever, saw a lady attend church without a hat and 'Sunday Best' was worn by men and women alike. Gradually hats have become optional, indeed seldom seen and casual clothing is commonly worn to church. In the last quarter-century the congregation have taken a greater part in church services – reading lessons, conducting prayers and assisting with Communion, all of which used to be done only by the vicar.

In 1992 St Peter's Church became united with St Thomas', Milnthorpe, Canon Hancock becoming vicar of both parishes. This was followed by the separate Mothers Union branches joining together in 1997. The Heversham branch had been in existence since 1922. The choir which had functioned for probably over a hundred years, and which, for over twenty years, had been a robed choir, was disbanded in the 1990s, although an 'ad hoc' choir comes together for sung evensong once a month and for other occasional singing.

St Peter's Church Choir was one of the first choirs to become a member of the English School of Church Music, later the Royal School of Church Music, and frequently joined with the other choirs in the district to sing festival services in Carlisle Cathedral and parish churches.

At a time when not many families had their own car, the annual choir outing was looked forward to with great anticipation. The Whitsuntide collection of £30-£40 in church was given to choir and this covered the coach hire charge (about £18 in the 1950s) and 10/- (50p) spending money for each choir member. We had some wonderful outings to Raby Castle, York, Blackpool, Southport, and even as far as Scarborough – all that way and not a glimpse of the sea due to a thick sea mist! Another trip in 1958 was to Wastwater, when the adventurous coach driver went further than the 'no coaches beyond this point' notice and inevitably got stuck. Fortunately, a number of grammar school boys were with us that year, and with much pushing and shoving by everyone, we got the coach onto firmer ground.

A Mother and Toddler Group was started by the Mothers' Union on 8th October 1980 and continues to meet in the Old School.

The church has been floodlit for many years over the Christmas period, but in 1999 permanent floodlighting was installed, partly to mark the Millennium and partly as a security measure. The new installation, which lights all four sides of the church and the steeple, was switched on by Sir Christopher Audland, from Ackenthwaite, on Christmas Eve. The Audland family have had a long association with the church and the lych gates were erected in 1894 by the sons and daughter of John Audland, who for thirteen years was a church warden. Sir Christopher Audland had been responsible for all the necessary planning, negotiating and overseeing of the scheme. A grant of 45% of the cost was made by the Millennium Commission and the balance paid for by the local Rhoda Thompson Trust.

The Trust arose under the will of Mrs Rhoda Thompson of The Knoll, in Woodhouse Lane. She left the residue of her estate (and her residence, for use as a Vicarage) for the benefit of the parish. The interest on the capital has been used to assist many different church and village projects.

Heversham Hotel 1930s. The hotel was unlicensed at the time. The licence and Blue Bell name were transferred soon after 1950.

CHAPTER SIX
THE CENTRE OF THE VILLAGE AND MARSH LANE

Opposite the church are some of the oldest houses in Heversham, with the exception of Rowangate, recently built on the site of some dilapidated outbuildings. The house next to it, Church View Cottage, was also the post office from 1872–1894.

Adjoining that house is Hawthorn Cottage, which was a small shop where almost any household item could be bought. This was run by Miss Mary Hogarth, affectionately known in the village as 'Auntie Polly'. This little shop was stocked to overflowing, leaving room for only about three customers. There was always a friendly welcome, and if an item was not in stock, Miss Hogarth always offered to get it. In earlier years the shop had been used jointly by Miss Hogarth and her sister Eleanor, as a dressmaking establishment. Mrs Brenda Sadler took over the premises later, making and selling an excellent variety of bakery products.

Next door is the present Post Office and shop. The Post Office could be found here during the years 1923-1930, then moved to No 1 Church Farm until 1979, when it moved back to this site. It has always been a friendly meeting place, continues to be so, and has also been the tuck shop to generations of boys and girls from the school.

The house next door is Sunnyvale and this was once long ago the site of the Ship Inn, although some historians think the next property, Chestnut House, was where the inn stood. Chestnut House has had a long history. It was so called after the two chestnut trees planted opposite in the churchyard in 1815, to commemorate the battle of Waterloo. It was the Grammar School headmaster's house in 1876 and a boarding establishment. It became a large family house occupied by my uncle and his family. During this time refreshments were served and accommodation offered for members of the Cyclists Touring Club. Later the building was made into three flats and later again into two separate residences as it is today.

In the beginning of the 20th century Heversham had only about twenty houses, mainly clustered around the church, while Leasgill had about thirty. During the century, housing in Heversham has increased to about one hundred and seventy-five and in Leasgill to sixty-three. Only four houses in the parish have been demolished during the century; two railway cottages in Woodhouse, a cottage in Rowell and the Toll Bar House.

Before moving on beyond the church, we look down Marsh Lane towards the

Centre of village. Chestnut House early 1900s when occupied by my Uncle Robert and his family. Cyclists were catered for and teas provided.

Heversham Hall - in the occupation of Handley family since 1876. People gathered for a 'Rogation Tide' service - held in May for the blessing of the forthcoming crops. Taken in 1980.

present Blue Bell. This was the vicarage until c.1843, then became a private house and remained so until the Princes Way was driven through the garden - which had previously extended up to the church corner and where the garden door can still be seen. By 1934 the premises had become, 'The Heversham Hotel', which was unlicensed, first run by Mr and Mrs Frank Dickinson, followed by other managers before the Chew family took over and ran the hotel for many years, the licence being transferred from the original inn around 1950 when the hotel also took the Blue Bell name.

Further down the lane are the old established farms of Heversham Hall and Moss Side. Heversham Hall, with its 14th century remains of a pele tower, is probably the oldest building in the parish and has been in the occupation of the Handley family since 1876. Successive generations of the family have been a strength to the farming community and to church and village life generally.

Beyond these farms the low-lying level ground on the right was the Brick Ponds. There is nothing now to show the location of that area of deep ponds, trees and undergrowth used as a site for depositing household waste. It was quite an attractive playground to boys in the early 1900s. Material for millions of bricks for the Hincaster canal tunnel was produced here in the early 19th century. The site was about two hundred yards above the small bridge over the drainage dyke and is now just a green field.

Above Heversham Grammar School
Below the laboratory, Heversham Grammar School - 1940s

Heversham Grammar School Old Boy's Collection

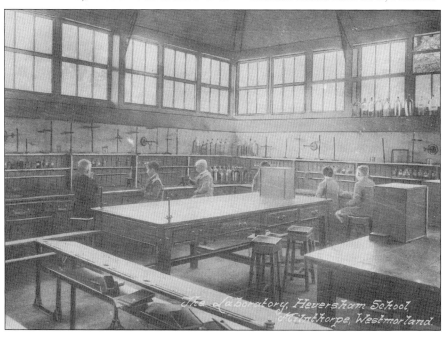

CHAPTER SEVEN
SOUTH FROM THE CHURCH

Returning to the village centre, a large barn once adjoined Chestnut House and this was demolished to make way for the residence now known as, 'Tower House'. Further building to the south took place around the turn of the last century, as far as Springfield - then two houses in separate occupation, but in the 1960s used together as boarding accommodation by the Grammar School. Several years ago the two houses were converted into six flats.

Leaving the church, on the east side of the road we come to numbers 1 and 2 Church Farm and Chestnut Cottage, now all private houses. Church Farm and the nearby outbuildings was a working farm, and Giles Whitwell came to farm there from Hutton Roof in 1915 and continued for many years. The Whitwell family have contributed much to village life. Mrs Whitwell took over the Post Office from Mrs Duncan at the village shop in 1930. Her daughter Mary then had the Post Office in her own name until she retired in 1979, when it went back to the shop then run by Russell and Jean Shuttleworth. They continued their good work there until nearly the end of the century, when Tony and Helen Rimmer took over. Mary and her sister Nancy (Tyson) were also the newsagents in Heversham, each delivering to homes in the village from 1948 to 1978. Nancy was Brown Owl, while her husband John was Scoutmaster.

The next three bungalows were built c.1928. Previously, a corner of this site was used by a travelling circus for a few years around 1925/6. This was an open-air circus ring and provided a night or two of excitement for those of us who were children at that time.

There have been tennis courts opposite Springfield for a number of years, but these were re-made in 1996 as the Heversham and Milnthorpe Tennis Club and the Milnthorpe Club closed. In partnership with Dallam School, a scheme for tennis coaching was introduced as a community effort for the school and village, and primary school pupils were also brought in for coaching.

Dallam School was established in 1984 when Heversham Grammar School and Milnthorpe Modern School were combined, thus bringing to an end the Grammar School status which had existed on this site since 1878, and since 1613 at the old Grammar School on Heversham Head, the one hundred and twenty-three metre high hill which overlooks the village on the east side. (*see page 57 for details of route to the top of Heversham Head from this point). There have been many improvements and extensions to the Heversham site in recent years.

The old 'fives court' remains, being one of very few in the district, and in my school days was in daily use for practice, and the senior and junior championships were an important event in the school's sporting year. The game is rather like squash but the ball is hit with the palm of the hand (or at some schools with a small bat). Sadly, the 'fives court' seems to have slipped into disuse, probably because most of the boys are based at the Milnthorpe site.

An important extra-curricular activity at the Grammar School was its Cadet Corps which functioned continuously from 1916. This was run on proper army lines with weekly drill periods, marching on the road, camping with the regular army and shooting practice in the purpose built rifle range. In my days at the school, the history master, Captain E C Worth, was in charge; later Vic Midgley took over, and other masters also gave their time to running the Corps. Several of the boys who passed through the Corps gave their lives in the 1939-45 war. An Air Force section was formed after the war, which had a very strong signals section. Soon after the merger with Milnthorpe Modern School the Cadet Corps was disbanded.

The school also had an excellent scout troop under the leadership of Mrs Nan Chinn. In October 1958 the troop had a demonstration of amateur radio transmission by Mr Guy Moser, a Kendal solicitor, as part of a worldwide "Jamboree on the Air". Mr Moser who lived in Oxenholme, was a keen amateur transmitter and helped the troop to exchange news with more than thirty amateur stations in fifteen countries, including Russia, The Vatican, Canada and Brazil, and the most distant exchange was with the Grapevine Troop in Texas, USA.

Some substantial new houses were built beyond the school in 1937/8 and in 1967/8 the Dugg Hill Estate came into being, increasing the size of Heversham by some forty-four houses.

Proceeding towards Milnthorpe we pass the driveway to Ellerhow (now called Tidal Reaches), built in 1916; the recently built Lawnswood; and Horncop built for Mr J F Curwen, architect and fellow of the Society of Antiquaries, occupied by him in 1900 and taking the name from his house in Kendal. Mr Curwen published the book "Heversham with Milnthorpe" in 1930. Other occupants followed, but it is interesting to remember that in wartime it was the home of evacuated Hull Girls' School. Some of the girls also boarded at the former residence of Canon Argles at Hawbarrow (almost next door and now called Hallbarrow) and at Chestnut House and Plumtree.

Barn dance (early 1990s) held in ancient cruck barn - Park House.

Heversham Station. The approach was down a driveway on the west side of the road, not many yards beyond the entrance to Horncop (Mass Transfer). There was a bell at the top to summon the station master to collect luggage.

'Kendal Tommy'. A Furness railway train stopped at Heversham Station. The date of the photograph is before 1907. The station master and a group of local dignitaries are welcoming a person thought to be Princess Alice, about to alight from the carriage. She was the daughter of HRH Prince Leopold, the 4th son of Queen Victoria.

The girls and their teachers regularly attended services in St Peter's Church. Eventually the house became office accommodation for the firm, Mass Transfer International.

The houses on the west side of the A6 as we leave the village were built in the second half of the 20th century, except Fairmead which was built c.1920 by Mr E J Abbatt. We pass the entrance to Park House Farm with its ancient 'cruck barn'. This was a primitive form of building construction sometimes used to support the roof of barns. This consisted of pairs of rough hewn timber beams arched and joined at the top end to provide a framework for the roof. Barn dances were occasionally held here by kind invitation of farmers, Gordon and Mary Capstick. These were really joyful events. We next come to the site where Heversham station stood. The entrance was a sloping drive from the road nearly opposite the drive to Horncop. The station opened in 1890 and trains ran from Grange to Kendal via Hincaster junction. Boys from Grange and Arnside used the train to travel to the Grammar School, and girls from Heversham and district boarded the train (in the days before buses) to get to Kendal High School. The train was nicknamed "Kendal Tommy".

This stretch of railway was part of the Furness line centred on Barrow and much used for passenger and goods traffic. Our Sunday School treats often consisted of a train journey from Heversham to Sandside or Arnside and thence on foot to the Fairy Steps in Beetham for a picnic. On occasions, the Royal Train was halted overnight on the line when Royalty were visiting the Furness peninsula. Passenger services ceased in 1942 and the line was finally closed in 1963.

The Eagle Temperance Hotel, Woodhouse Lane - 1950s

CHAPTER EIGHT
WOODHOUSE LANE

Now we return to the centre of the village for another diversion to Woodhouse Lane. In the beginning of the 19th century, on the left, was the Eagle & Child Inn - a licensed pub until 1908 when it became the Eagle & Child Temperance Hotel. In 1911 it was taken over by James and Elizabeth Allen and run by them for about forty years. Around the 1920s the Allen's daughter, Sylvia, ran a taxi service, driving a model T Ford, and although Heversham had a railway station by this time, buses had not arrived, and the taxi service was much appreciated. I remember my family being driven from Leasgill to Sedgwick to visit our grandparents. As we neared Heaves Hotel rain began to fall and we had to stop and put the hood up!

One room in the inn (looking into the churchyard) had a billiards table and this was for many years the headquarters of the Heversham Social Club. The club came into being in the early 1900s and continued until about 1967, by which time the building had ceased to be a hotel and had become a private house. The billiards table was stored for some years but eventually was fully restored by Reardon's of Blackpool and moved to the new snooker room, at the Athenaeum when the club opened in October 1994.

On 5th February 1982 the Eagle & Child was purchased from the Executors of Thomas Burrow for £650, on behalf of the Vicar and Churchwarden's Trust. It was intended at the time to establish a new village community centre, but this fell through, mainly because government grants for that kind of project ceased. When the tenant finally vacated the premises they were sold by the Trust to developers, who transformed the buildings into the four houses in 1995/6.

At the turn of the last century the only other house in Woodhouse Lane apart from The Eagle & Child was The Cottage, with a barn filling the space between. The barn was demolished in the 1950s. There were no other houses until we come to Sunnyside, near Tristrams playing field. Now both sides of the road are almost fully built up. The first house to be built was probably High Meadows in 1915, followed by Creggans and the Vicarage (in 1917); Whinfell and Hillside had been built by 1927. The remainder followed in various years leading up to 1999, when the last two were built on land which was owned by the Rhoda Thompson Trust.

Tristrams has been the school playing field during the whole of the 20th century and before. For much of that time it was the scene of rugby or cricket matches (or practice) on Thursday and Saturday afternoons. We went to school on Saturday mornings in those days. The annual Sports Day was also a great event. Heversham Head adjoining Tristrams was the site of Heversham Golf Club which flourished for a few years around the mid 1930s, when the Milnthorpe solicitor, J K Jackson was secretary.

The hamlet of Woodhouse outwardly does not appear to have changed much, apart from the building of the Haverwood houses from 1968 onwards and two or three other houses. The 'big house' was converted into three after Miss Elizabeth Lloyd (twenty-one years president of the Womens Institute) and her sister left to live at Bryn Avon on Princes Way. I remember Bridge House being a small sweet shop and there were two railway cottages near the main line railway bridge, which were demolished some years ago.

CHAPTER NINE
INTERESTING POINTS AND PLACES

HEVERSHAM HEAD (WALK REFERRED TO ON PAGE 49)

A walk to the top of Heversham Head is rewarded by a wonderful panoramic view - one thing which has hardly changed over the century. To the south-easterly direction one can see Ingleborough and turning clockwise the Kent Estuary, Whitbarrow Scar and the Lakeland fells. To reach the summit take the public footpath through the churchyard, leaving by the small metal gate. Climb past the old Grammar School building on the right, and enter the Head through the 'kissing gate', noting the cockpit on the right and continue upwards crossing the wall separating the low Head from the high Head by one of the two stiles - either to the right or left.

Having completed the walk in the village, a few more observations may be of interest.

TREES

The chestnut trees in the churchyard have already been mentioned; two old elm trees on the east side of the church had to be felled and a cedar tree was planted. At each side of the path through the churchyard leading to the Head are cherry trees planted in the late 1950s, in memory of Reverend Wilfred Cleghorn and his wife. Other cherry trees were planted (date uncertain) in the upper part of the churchyard by Mrs Ellwood, one time resident at Horncop.

A very large walnut tree used to grow within the walls of Heversham House on the north side. This regularly bore a good crop of walnuts and it was a pity that it had to be felled to make room for the present fire escape. The good news is that two other walnut trees have been planted – one mentioned below and the other, grown from a sapling raised in the parish, now in the children's playground. Neither seems to have produced fruit as yet.

In the grass area adjoining Dallam School car park the Parish Council planted a number of trees, including whitebeam, an English oak, a red oak, a walnut, a sycamore and a cherry. Most of these survived and are becoming mature trees. The avenue of trees along Princes Way was planted soon after the road was opened and has greatly altered the view of the village (especially the Leasgill end) as they have grown to maturity. Some died from Dutch Elm Disease but replacements were planted.

'Farmers Wife' played by Heversham Village Players in 1929 production.
Back row, left to right:- Herbert Kilshaw, James Sisson (my father), Sylvia Allen, Harry Sisson (my uncle) William Head (my cousin) Jean Tarves, John Handley, James Duncan,
Florrie Barlow, Frank Varley, Mary Whitwell, Norman Kilshaw and John Walker.
Middle:- Violet Gibson, Norah Varley, Albert Howson, Mrs N Chapman, Mrs Mabel Iremonger (producer), Olive Wild, Mary Procter and Gordon Birkett.
Front:- Marjorie Shepherd, (? not known), Joan Hanson and Edward Sisson The bright photographer's flash bulb has apparently caused many of the cast to close their eyes.

An example of how developing trees change the scene can be seen at Hallbarrow (Hawbarrow) – the trees now obscure the house, which in the early years of the last century could be clearly seen.

ENTERTAINMENT

In the early part of the last century, people in the village made their own entertainment. The Athenaeum was used frequently for whist drives and dances. Dancing was usually to a single piano player, or piano and drums, and occasionally with the addition of a violinist. No discos then! Whist drives and dances were the main fund raising events at that time – in more recent years coffee mornings have taken this function.

We had a variety of lectures, often with lantern slides projected from a large 'magic lantern', the light coming from an incandescent mantle through the burning of pressurised methylated spirits. Slides were then generally black and white on glass 3¼ inch square.

The Heversham Women's Institute have used the Athenaeum since its formation in 1927 and there were concerts and plays produced by the Guides and Brownies which were always a popular event.

A badminton club was formed in 1932 and has continued ever since. The main club now meets in Dallam School, but groups still play in the Athenaeum. More recently, indoor bowling has been a great success.

The years from about the mid 20s to the mid 30s were an outstanding period when the Heversham Village Players put on quite lavish stage shows – sometimes nearly half the village were in the cast! The performances received coverage in the national press and included notable titles as 'Tilly of Bloomsbury', 'Yellow Sands', 'The Farmer's Wife' and 'Precious Bane'. During the war years Mr Pearson who lived in part of Springfield, and his nephew, both evacuees from Kent, arranged excellent pantomimes. By all accounts they were 'not to be missed', but unfortunately, being in the RAF, I did not see them. In 1944 the pantomime was Dick Whittington.

Another long running activity is Old Time and Sequence Dancing. The original club ran for many years, but was wound up recently and taken over by another group which still continues weekly meetings.

In 1948 the then headmaster of Heversham Grammar School, Mr Norman Dawson, and his wife, Cora founded the South Westmorland Stage and Screen Society. A talented group of players put on first class performances in Big School, the large hall which was originally two separate class rooms and their first production being 'Grand National Night'. The society continued for many years using the school for their headquarters, and as well as plays, films were shown regularly. The society produced two films itself in conjunction with the school, 'More Than a Match' and 'Alice in Wonderland'. After some years the Society moved to its own premises, now called The Heron Theatre, in Beetham and continues to flourish there.

CELEBRATIONS

Heversham people have always celebrated Coronations, Royal anniversaries and other special events. In 1911, when the Coronation of King George V and Queen Mary took place, there was a long procession from Leasgill to Tristrams, headed by a brass band. Garlands were carried and there was a general sense of fun and jollity. Sporting events were held at Tristrams and presumably teas provided. In the evening there was the largest ever bonfire on Heversham Head.

The end of the First World War was celebrated with fireworks on the Head. In 1935 the Silver Jubilee of King George V and Queen Mary was again marked by a large bonfire, as was the Coronation of King George VI in 1937.

The end of the Second World War saw the beginning of the present children's sports, then under the title of Victory Celebrations. After a church service, sports were held on Haysteads field with refreshments in the Athenaeum, and a bonfire and fireworks at night. The event continued in this way for some years under the auspices of the Parish Council, but now a separate committee of mums and dads run the day, and the event is held on Bottom Pitch at Dallam School.

For the crowning of our present Queen in 1953 most houses were decorated in red, white and blue, with a prize for the best, won by Mrs L Lister at Leasgill Cottages. On the 50th anniversary of VE Day another bonfire and singsong were held on the lower Head.

TRANSPORT

Transport has been mentioned in relation to buses and trains, but before these arrived people walked or cycled to nearby destinations. Very few houses had a car (or horse and trap) in the early part of the last century. When I was a boy nearly every child walked to school whatever the weather; a few older children had bicycles. The roads were then much safer with little traffic and molesters were unheard of. Children usually walked in groups, as they did from Hincaster to the Primary School, the older children taking care of the younger ones.

In the early days the roads were not tarmacadamed (this was probably done

George VI Coronation Bonfire 1937. Left to right - Jim Sisson, Jean Simpson, Edith Binnie, Lesley Dobson, Oliver Simpson, Jean Binnie, Margaret Howson, B Dobson, Ena Bousfield, Billy Dawson, Frank Senogles, John Birch and John Dawson.

Jean Simpson

Jennie Sisson (my wife) outside our house, Leasgill Lodge, with our three sons, Ian on the left, Michael and Robin at the gate. Houses decorated for crowning of Queen Elizabeth in 1953.

Elephant Caravan coming along the main road past Church Farm - late 1800s

about 1915) and could be either very dusty or very muddy. There is reference in Parish Council minutes for 1907 to the dust nuisance and a further reference in 1908 for a substance called 'Dustabato' to be applied to the roads. It is not clear whether this was liquid or some form of granules. However, the problem continued, as again in 1915 there was another request by the Parish Council for spraying, or for the roads to be properly tarmacadamed. There were, of course, a considerable amount of animal droppings, which were scraped and brushed into tidy heaps by the roadside, and the occupants of houses nearby were eager to collect the heaps for use as garden manure.

The coming of the Westmorland section of the M6 in 1970 made a great difference to road traffic in the village. When the A6 carried all the heavy transport as well as commercial and private cars there were many hold-ups on Princes Way. On Sunday evenings particularly motor cars returning from a day out in the Lake District formed long tailbacks. Some tried to beat the queues which formed by taking the village road and the narrow lanes leading from it.

SHOPPING

The way we do our shopping has changed radically in recent years. Fortunately Heversham still has its village shop but so much shopping is now done at supermarkets. Gone are the days when most of the goods were brought to our door. One or two retailers still come round with vans and most of us are very glad the milkman and paperman come round daily, and the coalman from time-to-time. Contrast this with the days when we had a dozen or so salesmen calling regularly. Some of these I remember are:-

From Kendal we had:-

Bob and Jack Mackereth (butchers)

Louis Brennand (pork butcher)

Mr Geldart (baker)

We also had Eric Teasdale, from Booths, taking orders for groceries to be delivered in a day or two.

Dan Daly from Watson Brothers (clothiers)

Joe Richardson from Taylors Chemists - he came by train and carried a large suitcase of remedies

We had Mr Longcake the fishman from Flookburgh

From Milnthorpe we had:-

Mrs Gilham, selling cakes and pastries

Milnthorpe Co-Operative - Jimmy Prickett and other travellers came for orders

Joseph Daffady, selling shoes

Mr Proctor selling poultry food, from Pyes, producers of animal foodstuffs, who had mills at Beetham and Milton

We also had two carriers' carts served the village. These were horse-drawn vehicles rather like covered wagons. One was owned by Edward Clark and the other by Harold Hyde. Each made journeys from Milnthorpe to Kendal two or three times a week and delivered all manner of goods. Household items could be ordered from Kendal shops to be collected by the carrier and delivered to homes en route to Milnthorpe.

Householders often kept a few poultry and when eggs were plentiful in March and April, some were often preserved in a large earthenware crock in a liquid called, waterglass. This sealed the shells and eggs, they then could be kept for many months.

Also in those days before freezers, fruit from the garden was bottled in sugar syrup and sterilized by heat treatment. This still happens on a small scale mainly for show purposes.

There was also a man from Nelson in Lancashire who brought lengths of silk and cloth. He was a very welcome caller, especially at the time materials were scarce in wartime. We even had the ragman collecting worn out and cast off clothing, and there were various hawkers selling haberdashery and the like. Also, not so welcome, quite a few tramps begging for food.

One colourful character who appeared two or three times a year was the Breton onion man, generally carrying strings of onions on his bicycle handlebars.

Not all these listed above came weekly, most did, but some called monthly or at other intervals. So much shopping was done in a friendly way on the doorstep, hardly practicable now since so many wives are working in the day, but if internet shopping becomes popular will there be a reversal of going out to shop?

STREET LIGHTING

A feature which sharply divided the whole village, but which eventually changed the scene after dark was the installation of street lighting. This was first raised at a Parish Council meeting in 1949, but it was not until 1956 that work on the project was begun. This was after lengthy discussions about the pros and cons, particularly after a packed meeting in 1954 when considerable opposition was voiced. It was felt by some that street lighting would 'townify' the village; others thought that going out in the evening would be safer and less scary. This view eventually won the day and the lighting has proved a real boon. At first there were eleven lights, but others have been added over the years. I don't think anyone would like to be without the street lights now.

FARMING

There have been many changes in the farming scene. There used to be eighteen working farms in the parish with its present boundaries; now these have been reduced to eight. The farms which have been converted to private dwellings, together with their barns and outbuildings are – Eversley Farm, Waterside, Mabbin Hall, Bank Farm, Church Farm, Spout House, High House, Deepthwaite Farm, High Haverflatts and Lower Haverflatts.

Many men were employed on farms, some from the village and some hired at hiring fairs, but from the 1950s mechanisation caused numbers to dwindle and now much of the work is undertaken by contractors. Most farms sold milk and butter direct from the premises. Farmers' wives took a large part in the physical work on the farm and children were sometimes kept away from school to help with potato harvesting etc.

There has been quite a change of scene through upgrading pasture land by clearing wild flowers, bracken and gorse, but visually this is not so pleasing. Large areas of Heversham Head were covered with bracken and gorse which were a joy to behold but this is nearly all gone now.

On the other hand the roadway 'lengthmen' who cut the verges regularly and kept the roadside tidy are no longer employed and wild flowers grow again (sometimes overhanging the road thus obscuring the view and reducing safety).

Some farmers now supplement their income by providing bed and breakfast for holidaymakers; pick-your-own fruit fields and by having caravan sites on their land. A big change for the low-lying farms has been the prevention of flooding. Over a long period of time work has been done to strengthen the banks of the River Kent and the estuary and so it is unlikely that fields will be entirely flooded as they were in the earlier years of the last century.

The Westmorland Gazette dated 23rd March 1907 had big headlines and gave much space to the disastrous gale and tidal flood, which occurred on the night of 16/17th March. The river banks from Levens to Sandside on the left bank and from Levens to Meathop Marsh on the right bank, burst with great loss of sheep and cows, and much damage to house and furniture. College Green was worst affected. Some cattle and horses were moved to Eversley,

Levens Hall, Lawrence House, Ninezergh and Low Levens. The flood also affected Halforth and Waterside, and Park House Farm suffered considerably.

THE PHOTOGRAPHS

Some of the pictures are from my own collection and some from those given or lent to me over the years. Quite a number are from old postcards bearing postmarks around 1908-1912. These were written by my father, (a joiner, wheelwright and undertaker), who lived in Leasgill, to my mother, (who learned dressmaking and did sewing for the Walker family at Brettargh Holt), who lived in Sedgwick, during their courting days. Dad would write a card in the morning making a date with Mum in the evening, post it in Heversham (old ½d stamp) and it would be delivered in Sedgwick the same afternoon. Who needed a mobile phone? Fortunately most of these old postcards have been preserved.

POSTSCRIPT 2000

The Millennium has arrived and was ushered in at a watchnight service in St Peter's Church. There were also parties and fireworks in the village.

A beautiful new Millennium banner now hangs in the church. This was designed and made mainly by Jean Sowerby and Margaret Hesmondhalgh, but members of the parish were invited to add their own stitches (under supervision!). No fewer than one hundred and seventy-one individuals took part. Their names are recorded on laminated sheets and incorporated between the front of the banner and its backing.

Another permanent Millennium feature is the panoramic indicator on Heversham Head. This stems from an idea put forward by the Parish Council after consultation with village people. The Heversham Church of England Primary School prepared a time capsule which was placed in the base of the structure on 12th April.

The lead capsule contained newspapers and magazines and twenty leaflets describing local attractions. There was also a letter addressed to 'Children of the Future' (from Class 2). Other items include:

School inspection reports, photos, staff/governors, term dates and handbooks

Coins, stamps, early counting apparatus, tea towel and sweatshirt

(many more items included)

The indicator is constructed of Burlington slate and special limestone from Horton-in-Ribblesdale, surmounted by artistically carved panels by Danny and Lara Clahane, from Kendal, depicting the distant scene. The first sod was cut by Hal Bagot of Levens Hall and Mrs Susan Bagot will officially unveil the indicator on 24th June.

Now we look forward to the Millennium Fun Evening in September. This event for all ages and all the village is to be held at Dallam School, Heversham site, organised by church members

THE NEXT 100 YEARS?

What will Heversham be like in the next 50 or 100 years? What will survive and what will disappear? Perhaps someone will keep a notebook – if so, do record the date with each item, photograph, etc. I have found confirming dates quite difficult.

Jean Sowerby (left) and Margaret Hesmondhalgh with the Millennium banner.   *By permission of Jean Sowerby*

Pupils from Heversham St Peters Church of England Primary School, burying items in a lead time capsule, in the foundations of a panoramic indicator on Heversham Head (12th April 2000). Head teacher Kath Fisher sitting on right, with chairman of parish council and Millennium Committee, Peter Johnson..

'photo courtesy of The Westmorland Gazette'

Class 1 (Teacher: Mrs K Fisher) Mrs Gorrigan and Mrs Shepherd (not shown) Samuel Willacy (absent), Sophie Fishwick, Kayleigh Jones, William McFadden, Katie Bedford (not shown), Sophie Thwaites-Breed, Holly Little, Thomas Davies, Jonathan Hyman, Daniel Hancock, Laura Hamer, Bronwen Salter, Eilish McDougall, Elouise Chambers, Adam Handley, Luke Jackson, Alice Pickthall, Katherine Atkinson, Holly Robinson, Tom Wheatley, Harrison Dobson, Alex Child, Jessica Pickthall, Ben Coates, Charlotte Thwaites-Breed, Jack Graham, Amy Fox.

Class 2 (Miss M Helliwell) Joseph Alaimo (not shown), Robbie Collinson, Emily Crowder, James Dootson (not shown), Richard Dowker, David Ely, Paul Gibson, Adam Lewis, Stuart Mason, Katy Medcalf, Harry Norman, Ashley Porter, Anna Sellars.

Class 3 (Mrs V Sanders) - not shown
George Alaimo (not shown), Oliver Dootson, Liam Ganncliffe, Nicholas Hamer, Steven Jackson, Melissa Little, Kayleigh Moffat, Rose Norman (not shown), Alexander Parsons, Jade Porter, Joanna Swinbank (not shown), Emma Chapman, Thomas Coates (not shown), Matthew Cummins, Benjamin Hamer (not shown), James Hyman (not shown), Thomas Inman, Emma Matthews, George Moffat, Douglas Parsons (absent), Thomas Sellars, Max Shaw (not shown), Scott Singleton (not shown), Laurence Stannard, Kirsty Tyson.

Class 4 (Mrs L Jopling) and Mrs Sisson (not shown)
Melissa Birbeck, Jessica Brabender, Stephanie Dowker (not shown), Grace Eden, Joseph Ganncliffe, Catherine Gunby, Jonathan Matthews, Lewis Remington, Elizabeth Salter (not shown), Heather Swinbank, Kimberley Warren, Stefan Brabender, Russell Cooper (not shown), Anne Fell, Adam Fox, Rebecca Hartley, Rebecca Inman, Emily Jackson, Simon Knight, Sara-Kay Martindale, Thomas Mason (not shown), Robert Matthews, Alasdair McHardy, Stuart Metcalfe, Meghan Moffat, Amie Hodgkinson, Steven Oversby (not shown), Bryony Shaw, Alexander Simm, Gary Singleton (not shown), Emma Stannard, Ross Stevenson, Mehan Whelan.